Raptor

PHOENIX POETS

ANDREW FELD

Raptor

THE UNIVERSITY OF CHICAGO PRESS

Chicago & London

ANDREW FELD is assistant professor in the Department of English at the University of Washington and editor in chief of *The Seattle Review*. He is the author of *Citizen*, a 2003 National Poetry Series selection.

The University of Chicago Press, Chicago 60637
The University of Chicago Press, Ltd., London
© 2012 by The University of Chicago
All rights reserved. Published 2012.
Printed in the United States of America

21 20 19 18 17 16 15 14 13 12   1 2 3 4 5

ISBN-13: 978-0-226-24039-8 (paper)
ISBN-10: 0-226-24039-8 (paper)

Library of Congress Cataloging-in-Publication Data
Feld, Andrew, 1961—
    Raptor / Andrew Feld.
        p. cm. — (Phoenix poets)
    ISBN-13: 978-0-226-24039-8 (paper : alk. paper)
    ISBN-10: 0-226-24039-8 (paper : alk. paper)
    I. Title. II. Series: Phoenix poets.
    PS3606.E385R37 2012
    811'.6—dc22   2011009328

♾ This paper meets the requirements of ANSI/NISO Z39.48-1992 (Permanence of Paper).

for LUKAS *and for* PIMONE

who made the life these poems came out of possible

in memory of my father, MAURY DAVID FELD

CONTENTS

ACKNOWLEDGMENTS

Grateful acknowledgment is due to editors of the following journals, where some of these poems first appeared:

American Literary Review: "Cascade Raptor Center: Capture" and "Post-Confessional"
Bat City Review: "After Johnny Carson's Final Appearance on *The Tonight Show*" (as "After Johnny Carson's Final Appearance on 'The Tonight Show'")
Free Verse: "Raptor" (p. 3), "The Test," and "Raptor: A Brief Lexicon"
Gulf Coast: "Quarters"
The Iowa Review: "Guide" (p. 14), "Guide" (p. 61), and "There"
The New England Review: "Tongue: An Ode" (as "Tongue")
Tikkun: "Visitant"

To Louise Shimmel, director, Lauren Huse, and the other staff and volunteers at the Cascade Raptor Center in Eugene, Oregon, where I received my hands-on education in the care and feeding of these astonishing creatures, and to the raptors I was "privileged to in extreme," I owe a debt, toward which I hope this book might be seen as a partial repayment.

I am also happily compelled to express my gratitude for the help provided by the first readers of this book: Rick Barot, Linda Bierds, Martha Collins, Robyn Schiff, and Nick Twemlow; and to Drs. McKay, Wood, and Engleberg. An Artist Trust Fellowship and a

University of Washington RRF Grant provided much-needed assistance in the completion of this work.

Many of these poems use quotations taken, with some corruption, from *The Art of Falconry: Being the De arte venandi cum avibus of Frederick II of Hohenstaufen*, written around 1250, translated and edited by Casey A. Wood and F. Marjorie Fyfe (Stanford: Stanford University Press, 1969).

The epigraph in part three is taken from *Hawks in the Hand: Adventures in Photography and Falconry*, by Frank and John Craighead (New York: Lyons & Burford, 1997).

For greater knowledge of and background information about the author of *The Art of Falconry*, I have drawn extensively on *Frederick the Second 1194–1250*, by Ernst Kantorowicz, translated by E. O. Lorimer (New York: Ungar, 1957), and the necessary corrective to his Nietzschean hyperbole, *Frederick II: A Medieval Emperor*, by David Abulafia (New York: Allen Lane, 1988).

One

We call raptorial all those birds who, employing their powerful flight and the special fitness of their members, prey upon any other bird or beast they are able to hold and whose whole sole sustenance is the flesh of such animals. These are the eagles, hawks, owls, falcons and other similar genera. They feed only upon their prey—never upon dead flesh or carrion—and are therefore called rapacious birds.

Among the characteristic forms of their organs may be mentioned: the beak, which in birds of prey is generally curved, strong, hard, and sharp, claws that are bent inward and are hard and needle-pointed; retracted eyes; a short neck, short legs, and the posterior toe of each foot very strong. The female is always larger than the male. Not all the foregoing is true of non-raptorial birds.

Functionally also they differ in that raptorials are more keen-sighted and have more acute hearing than other birds. They are strong in flight but walk badly. They dislike water and drink little, fly alone, and live long. They drive their young early from the nest and then abandon them; and this behavior is not that of nonrapacious birds.

The Art of Falconry, Emperor Frederick II of Hohenstaufen

RAPTOR

What I wanted was a goshawk on my wrist,
A docile bit of wilderness in my care.
Her setting-sun red eye returned my stare.
Inside the cage I am a nurse, waiter,
And janitor. Outside, an austringer.
I searched for one all day in the forest.
Now *Chiefly poet*. Now *Shakes*. Now *sing*. Now *rare*.

I searched for one all day in the forest
So I could cross the bird off my life-list.
At the Center I fed her as you hold this
Poem—at a reading distance. The flared
Warning of her red eyes refuted my stare:
You will *never* cross me off your life-list.
Now *Chiefly poet*. Now *Shakes*. Now *sing*. Now *rare*.

You wanted a little bit of wilderness
Held docile on your wrist. What could be tamer
Than extinct? At the trail head, the profiled picture.
If you see this bird, call our 800 number.
Because except what you allow me there
Is no wilderness, there is no wilderness.
Now *Chiefly poet*. Now *Shakes*. Now *sing*. Now *rare*.

CASCADE RAPTOR CENTER: CAPTURE

I'd sooner, except the penalties, kill a man than a hawk.
—Robinson Jeffers, "Hurt Hawks"

I.

He hadn't *meant* to hit the bird, he said
repeatedly, although not one of us
who had to mend the wing-shot hawk believed him.
We lifted the red-tail, half-dead with loss
of blood, out of the box she had arrived in
like a small mummy from a sarcophagus.
When she flicked the milky filters of her eyelids
I saw my shadow-shape projected across
a screen, grown representative and monstrous.

He *hadn't* meant to hit the bird, he said
stubbornly, as to convince himself, or us,
his punishment—to stay in the corner where
quails and rats defrosted in a trough
while his father waited out in the car
and we tried to keep alive the bird he shot—
was too severe, unjust. He hadn't intended
any injury, not even as he pulled
the trigger and watched it fall into his neighbor's field.

He hadn't meant to *hit* the bird, he said.
The gun, a birthday present, made the act seem
part of a ceremony: what better way
to mark the date of your arrival in
this world—the day was his eleventh birthday—
than by taking out a life? The hawk screamed
once as it fell from the distance where it lived
so far beyond the extension of his will
it seemed impossible to hit, or hurt, or kill.

He hadn't meant to hit the bird, and I
tried to follow the thought back to those fields
where nothing ever changes but the weather
and what the work of his farming neighbors yields.
The boredom that turns into a kind of fever.
The stirring inner life. He was still a child,
cornered, in fatigues, and trying not to cry
as we ignored him—if he'd killed a man we'd all
have been the more compassionate, the less appalled.

He hadn't meant to hit the bird. Who cared?
While we immobilized the broken wing
the boy stayed frozen in the corner where
his father told him to stay, his rat-tail dangling
limply into the rodent-like fine hairs
across his neck. There was internal bleeding.
With surgical tweezers we picked bone shards
and dirt out of the bullet hole, and went
about the careful business of his punishment.

II.

The silence arrived with them, full-blown and brittle,
                along with the hawk,
swaddled in a towel once white but now use-yellowed

and grained with green swaths of degreaser,
                then placed in a box
as per our instructions. As an instrument, blind

to the long-term results, we could only speak
                of the immediate effects,
which apparently were mutually punishing.

The image I have of them is the brick-red hood
                of their Subaru curving
past moss-covered rock faces on Route 126,

the two-lane highway leading like a fallen kite's string
                through McKenzie Bridge,
Blue River, Leaburg, Nimrod, Walterville, Thurston,

rural POs and gas stations shouldering up out of
                the fog then sinking
back under, to Springfield and Eugene where we

were prepped and waiting. I can't keep my mind
                out of the front seat.
In the rear of the Outback the high-school science

texts he teaches slide on their backs, open and riffling
          from biology to chemistry
and geology, the box full of bird in the back seat

a kind of case study as the estranged creature
          beside him hugs his
nylon chest strap and stares at the dash and he flips

through the little he knows of child psychology.
          He's driving too fast.
All the way there the McKenzie seethed on the left,

spring-fed rivulets muscled with melt, each tributary
          mouth frothing
where it met the river rising out of its bed and over

the top to those of us who prefer our aggression
          more passive. Water
that turbid is surface all the way to the bottom.

When I started this poem I was concerned
          with shame, that under-
current stretched between them, tensing the silence

which resumed in an altered pitch after the shot
          interrupted the flat fields
and echoed back like a second shooter and the hawk

slid down the sky screeching. I think the boy
          could use a little music.
He'd like to hear the thin mouth of the car stereo sing

a page or two from the Great American Songbook.
The father is still running
across the field. After the interrogation, anger

will twist the vise-like muscles of his jaw shut.
Inside are eddies
which at their base resolve into black circles

the same size and shape as the volume and tone knobs
on both sides of the stereo's
face. Just because the songs are minimal variations

on a few themes, bright gloss or rebuttal, doesn't mean
they're any less heartfelt.
They're still us. When the boy tried to turn the radio on

his father slapped his hand away, which was the only
time they touched
in the three hours it took them to drive from Redmond

to the Raptor Center. Even the self-winding voices
of talk radio would
have bound them to the familiar. Even unconscious,

a bit of froth in a furrow of the High Desert Country's
expanse, the red-tail,
a gorgeous pale morph, impressed both with the weight

of what it had fallen from and into. The little abysmal
            mark of its contact
with us near the right shoulder, bleeding. The father

couldn't breathe. The son didn't need to.

THE ART OF FALCONRY
for Pimone

Recalcitrant and hard to train, the haggard
goshawk clutches my wrist, the pattern on
his front like shadowed snow called mail: jesses,
      leash, and swivel, his bells
replaced by a telemetry device,
he images a sense-intelligence
wholly responsive to the summer field,
to him alive with switches turning on and off.

In hooded sleep the ornament he is
more than requites the disciplined patience
the passage bird caught beyond her second
      season demands; as in
any late-life marriage, instinct's awry
until rewired, as appetite provides
an access to that balance or accord
where difference defines itself by recognition.

Unblinded, each blink of his two-lidded eyes
admits another fraction into the scope
of his attention. The way you hear the day
      click into focus as he lifts
a lizard foot to test his jess then pliers it
around your thumb is fucking *awesome,* as is
the release of when you throw him to the winds.
Hidden in reeds, a goldfinch shifts to full alarm.

The straps and husbandry, the exercise
of wills chafing at limit, pricing cartons
of beef and chicken stock at the QFC,
        as in nostalgia's cost-
ineffective false binary the goshawk
follows with love and active heat the game:
drawn to the lure of a shared diet, we wait
for love's connecting strings to latch onto the kill.

Since marriage is a form of making, some days
we're lightning-struck. Others, faculty meetings.
In the kitchen reeds and switchgrass click as the dish-
        washer, that excellent
machine, thrums through the stages of its mimic
intelligence—*soak, scrub, rinse*—and in the moment
the machine allows for us, I hover above
you, stalled by an imperative wider than thought.

The field grows distant. Then closer than ever.
From below the creased topography of our sheets
a sleep leaches up to claim us, against appetite,
        which only sharpens on
the whetstone of you. The blinds are back down.
There is a gravity, a weight, to each
word we allow into this intimacy, here,
before silence clamps its open mouth over us.

THE WORK

"Birds of prey have no song." — James Richardson

This happened on my first day there. Class,
pay attention. The bird was bronze, pine-mulch
brown and beaten copper wire, not golden. Think
before you speak. Much can be conveyed
through tone. The eagle's voice was sampled
from *Metal Machine Music,* an album that can
drive roaches out of your apartment. It's good
to think of music as having a function, praise,
or lament, satire or warning. It's good to think.
Never walk in front of an unhooded eagle.
Remember, experience is a dim lamp
which illuminates only the one who carries it.
Wearing a little leather cap and held tightly
between my upper arms, the eagle was as if
asleep: it was like holding a baby swaddled
in razor wire, although size and the caution
accorded to the useless wing made the experience
for me a very *Pietà* kind of thing. God, won't you
pay attention? When a raptor has been injured
so it no longer can survive in the wild we call
that condition educational, which doesn't mean
it's tame. To trim the talons, fully extend
the leg, and the muscles will pull the foot open.

There is the small glee we feel in the presence
of elegant machinery, which is separate
from its function. Use dog-nail clippers
for the claws, for the beak a small power-sander
like hobbyists use on dollhouses. The similarities
between Ren Faires and wildlife rehabilitation
are more than a shared love of leather gauntlets
and Elizabethan terminology, and some of these birds
are named for Tolkien's elves, which is kind of
embarrassing? Another function is to encase
the significant moment in amber although here
they use 2x4s and chicken wire. Back under
her Plexiglas roof, Eowyn is a thought followed
to its complete, unhappy conclusion. Think
of Schoenberg's emancipation of dissonance, of
Ornette Coleman and all 17 minutes of "Sister Ray."
Expand your definition of song. Avoid aphorism.

GUIDE

With spring there came that sense of clarity
*   we'd missed all through the rainy months, although*
the somnolescent clouds still held their ground;
*   the change was slow and what we felt was less*
the promise of enameled days or that
*   love's blade might strike the jetting vein again*
than that the bulk of days had shifted in a new
*   direction, away from us, as the sky thinned.*

In March I heard Louise in her office
    above the visitors' center haranguing
her forestry contact about the lack
    of useful information on their website;
then, descending from the flight cage, I found
    four deer legs the funny state troopers left
propped at a standstill in the gauzy mist
    as if they had outrun their animal.

A cold wisp licked the back of my neck as I
    considered how the bureaucracy that owns
our birds from molt to tail feather compensates
    for the lack of any central intelligence
with a kind of wit barbed with malevolence.
    I wrapped the road-killed legs in plastic bags
and buried them deep in the outdoor freezer.
    It was like that: the vibrant image, the aftermath.

Days spent crawling under shrieking kestrels
     to scrub out their whitewashed black plastic tub
or in a crabbed dance with our ferruginous hawk
     scrunching away on his Astroturf-covered perch,
keeping as much distance as his small cell
     allowed between us as if by mutual
agreement—although our only *mutual*
     is the tethering hunger we use to bind our birds

to us and overcome their deep-rooted
     abhorrence of the human face, *dreadful*
to her as to all other animals.
     Always, *the face of man is the lion's face.*
As our almost-eagle stretched out a wing
     like a broken comb, I felt again the shame
of an instinctive reaction to the power-
     lessness of love rebounding on its object.

Outside the rotting salmon dumpster-stink
     which seemed to issue from our osprey's wound
and filled her cage, or where our turkey vulture
     Lethe pecked at the exposed veins that are
my bootlaces, the spring flowers bloomed out
     a counterpoint, white petals of Trillium
echoing the green, Star-Flowered Solomon's Seal,
     Indian Plum and the Red-Flowering Currant.

You know how any practiced speech becomes
     theatrical?—so the rote recitals of
my guide talk turned my voice into a stranger's
     leading you through the small cell of my self-

consciousness, a voice at odds with its subject,
      ingratiating, *false*—and these cages
only numbered and labeled boxes in
      the warehouse where they're storing the disaster.

Then the little difference between the dead
      bird in my hand and the one with a yellow eye
aimed at my handful of quail narrowed to nothing
      and I became elegy's functionary.
Brown-veined petals of the Yellow Wood Violet,
      deep rose flowers of the Salmonberry,
Star-Flowered Solomon's Seal, Indian Plum,
      Red-Flowering Current and Western Trillium.

Here is my day: a drawer of mice I shake
      to keep excessive life from spilling out
then slide in the asphyxiating oven.
      The resigned feet entering the beak, the tail
curlicuing into a question mark, as if
      still curious of what it entered into.
An owl with one eye cataracted blind,
      the other bright with purpose, focused beyond,

to where the netted shadows of the state
      forest fall on the bright borders of our
groomed lawns and trails. At my shift's end the sky
      also locks down, and in the old growth trees
surrounding us a wooing, hooing voice
      evades its source as we listen, trying
to draw shades of meaning between the call
      and its corresponding, captive answer.

We like to think they call each other out
of love, which we find sweet; what weirds us out
is not the great horned male moving inside
 the light-excluding heights just outside our
borders, his voice always one flight removed
 from the still-trembling throat we feel as ours,
become the body of his audience,
 or how it brings our half-blind female awake

to the extreme of her confinement, clambering up
 the chicken wire; but how they start calling
too late, too late *to each other before*
 it's registered on us as dark, and I'm
still busy with my tasks—so much, this late,
 impossible to finish, down on my knees
with a handful of pellets grained with mice teeth
 and vertebrae, smaller and finer than life.

VISITANT

Blown off course here by an errant trade wind, the bird
Perched on a forbidding sign and preened Eurasian mites
From its barred caudal feathers, onto our soil. In this
Unstable weather we're having of late, the crocus splits
Open in March and spills its bright whites, yellows, and
Purples in a late-winter warmth we'd call unseasonable
If that word didn't sound so archaic now; and borne on
Uncalendared winds, these accidentals arrive as trouble's
Sparks spinning in the auto-da-fé we're making of our
Planet. A New World grasshopper dead in one red talon,
The falcon exhibits a perfect equanimity at the Cessna's
Unsteady landings on the sand-islanded airstrip behind
Its taxiway perch, as perfection's what the bird's all
About, the balance between energy consumed and expended
Calibrated on a scale so precise, subject to a killing
Economy, each strand of the swing feathers' dark leading
Edge and pale puffy white bars of the underwing coverts
Is weighed and measured. In answer to the falcon as an
Image of the soul, or of the desiring mind in flight, I
Offer the carved image of the martyr, Saint Gorgonius,
Ca. 1500, a missal in his slightly elevated right hand
As a falcon grips his gloved left fist, forearm held at
A right angle, in the proper position, as the as-yet un-
Decided noble hesitates between our world and the next.
The falcon is the world. If the saint views his prayer
Books' open pages through half-shut, heavy-lidded eyes,

As one trembling for touch shuts down one sense to make
Another more acute, the bird on his hand has the disked
Pupils of a predator waiting for an error, the pause or
Extra wing-beat as a quail hesitates between escape routes,
Any of the little lapses of attention the falcon preys
On. Once, driving too fast to Vermont to visit a girl-
Friend, my car spun out on a corner of the interstate's
Iced-over mountain roads, pinballing between guardrails
At 60 mph instinct and thought whirled uselessly around
The abyss between my abdomen and lungs until I pillowed
Into a snowbank. So the young aristocrat surrenders to
Historical drift and under the eagle standard of empire
Lets slip the falcon's jess, choosing instead the quail
Life and fate. And his end was terrible, according to
The law which says that who an emperor loves must be as
Broken as the fall from such height dictates. His sides
Were curried with iron combs and the sinews of his left
Leg cauterized. Forefinger roughly knuckling the worn-
Bronze spear-points on ermine-white breast of his hybrid
Peregrine-gyrfalcon, the falconer said: These birds are
Not pets, disgorging a pellet. Once out of nature, you
Can't get back and are home only in an increasingly in-
Tricate cage. Even among our socks-and-sandals fellow-
Ship of nerdy birders some believe the salt marsh dawn
Provides a requisite opacity, a mistiness which enhances
By obscuring the bird's singularity, as if all beauty's
Best air-brushed, but my 10 x 42 Zeiss Victory FL's bring
Me to the falcon's perch faster than Keats' imagination
And closer. O phase-corrected, mirror-free prisms! and
O the fully multi-coated lenses' blue-black mid-Atlantic
Depths, gold-suffused and seen through to the juvenile

Molt on its boldly barred primaries. O pale cheeks and
Buffy nape, yellowish slate beak, and the pebbled red-
Orange leather of its cere and feet—and between, O it's
Infuriating—its wind-smudged gray breast will not focus
Itself as the bird swoops and stops above the moldering
Suede cattail tips, like a smear on the air's glass all
My expensive German optics can't quite resolve, although
To see it sharply is all I would ever ask of this world.

THE ART OF FALCONRY
for Linda Gregerson

I. AFTER RILKE

Being boy-emperor means keeping the crown
in an unspecified location, a tower
rising brick by brick in the secret architecture
of a larger design; so when secretaries found

him—kingly, adult—on the second floor
of the Apulian lodge, saying into an early
recording device the treatise *De arte venandi
cum avibus,* a scribe bent over

his unadorned Latin, their fears of a distempered
reaction to another piece of papal blackmail
were misplaced—as boy he knew the protocol:
keep your head bowed before your elders

and count slowly to sixty, before signing
the death sentence, as if still burdened
by responsibilities already mastered in
the royal schoolhouse of the womb. Nothing

touches him, except this unsettled, unseeled
creature, an all-white gyrfalcon, on his wrist.
As he paced out the night, her unstitched
eyes adjusting to strange, new sights, and the feel

of that hand's gentle strokes, whatever required
him—treaties, crusades, matters of state
begging for execution—would wait
on who is in himself the state, until the gyr-

falcon, "lord or chief of falcons," at his command
rose through the all-embracing morning, carrying him
too aloft, until it dropped down on the heron—
a radiance released by, and then returning to, his hand.

II. FREDERICK II OF HOHENSTAUFEN (1194–1250)

Who was the King of Sicily and Jerusalem, Holy Roman Emperor, and author of *De arte venandi cum avibus,* or *The Art of Falconry,* "the first zoological treatise written in the critical spirit of modern science."

Who was called *Stupor Mundi,* The Wonder of the World.

Whom Nietzsche called "the first European" and "one of my nearest kin."

Whom Dante placed in hell with the Epicureans, "who make the soul die with the body."

Who had a man imprisoned in a perfectly tight-fitting wine vat and left to perish, to demonstrate that the soul which could not escape from the vat must have perished with the body.

Who had a number of infants reared by nurses who were forbidden to speak to them, to discover whether the children could speak Hebrew, or Greek, or Latin, or Arabic as the original of all languages, or whether they would speak the speech of their parents who had borne them. The experiment failed when all the children died.

Who, to discover which of two men had better digested his food, the one who had rested after his meal or the other who exercised, had both cut open to see.

Whose aim, in *De arte venandi cum avibus,* in reproof of Aristotle and other authorities, was "to show those things that are, as they are" (*manifestare ea que sunt, sicut sunt*).

Who, when the great khan of the Mongols told him to submit to his might or forfeit his crown, replied that he might gladly resign his throne if he were allowed to become the khan's falconer.

Who tried to determine whether birds of prey detect their quarry by sight or smell. "We have often experimented in various ways. For when falcons are completely blinded (by stitching the eyelids) they do not even detect the meat that is thrown to them, though nothing impedes their sense of smell."

Whose passion for the chase cost him the gravest defeat of his career, when outside Parma the emperor heard, over his falcons' silver bells, the great alarm bell of Victoria, and returned to the battle too late. Lost fifteen hundred men, his treasury, his menagerie, his eunuchs, and his harem.

In whose court was founded Italian lyric poetry, limited entirely to the subject of love, and generally expressed in gentle, unexaggerated tones.

THE GAME

Mea culpa: when the candidate explained
dressing up on weekends as an SS officer as
"a father/son bonding thing," I wanted to kill him.

There's a hole I go down then, with walls
so close I can feel a damp hand or rubber mask
clamped over my nose and mouth to smother me

in my own exhaust and saliva. At this level,
you watch as etched crystal-work gears shatter
and adhere under the chocolate-bar tread patterns

these weekend war-buffs walk though
the stubbled fields on. At this level, rabbit
ears are fuzzed stalks trembling in a dry wind

and the rabbit is also a plant. The candidate
explained the uniforms are historically accurate
in all respects but out of respect for our sensitivities

they removed the swastikas, as if to say
these soldiers who surround you are armed
with cap-firing, replica weapons, so don't worry

my son, my seed, stalk and flowering
American exception—their guns are loaded
with blanks, blank too the disk the eagles on

their daggers now grip, a black hole
Jews, Gypsies, Communists, and the men
who love each other all disappeared down,

pulled by a gravitational force so fierce
the idea of us follows us into the erasure
of this open space, state park, or playing field

edged with foxglove, scotch broom
and blindweed. Although his campaign
failed, the candidate is still primed for other

battles. It's surprising, he says, how
real his replica MP40 Schmeisser machine
pistol looks and feels, how with no stoppages!

in full automatic firing mode, the Plug
Fire Cartridges create movie-like muzzle-
flash and real recoil, but I'm not surprised.

To me, the real-like firing smoke after
empty shells are ejected smells worse than
like if not as bad as real and serves as an index

of the heat and compositional fire
from pyres of books burned before they
could be written and I am not writing this.

Two

LITTLE VIRAL SONG

Always the fear was the infection
Would shift from them to us.
So the sad piles of chicken flesh
In West Timor and Bangladesh
Gave us that certain, sad frisson
One feels near the apocalypse.

One feels, near the apocalypse,
A little less than one—
A chill you can warm your hands on.
As the infection zeros in
From the East, one feels jaundiced.
The end *would* come from that direction.

The end will come from that direction
One is already inclined
Toward. In suburban Maryland,
The epicenter of my mind,
The die-off of the crows and ravens
Made me think: even here? in Kensington?

And even here in Washington
State, we watch them, shivering
Inside the zero's open eye
Of our wide-screen television
(They are sick, they must die) (and no birds sing).
So long to the great wingèd migration.

So long to the great wingèd migration:
Now harbinger, instead
Of spectacle of the world's renewal.
What should the likes of us do,
Crawling between toilet and bed?
And there are other, worse, symptoms.

Among the other, worse, symptoms
Is an embarrassing
Tumescence, the chthonic thrill
Of apocalyptic porn, the chill.
One feels the zero homing in.
Always, the fear is the infection.

QUARTERS

I.

Pouring a plastic baggie's worth down the Coinstar's
gullet, the 9.8% tax on my laziness gladly paid to hear
the jingling sounds, the chatter and metallic shake
of change, the nuisance of it lessened to a slip I take
to the cashier, I watch each little state slide by:
the blind woman of Alabama, Hawaii's
native king, the horses of Wyoming, Kentucky, Nevada, Delaware,
the horned skull of Montana, Alaska's bear
eating a salmon, the buffalos and cows of North Dakota, Wisconsin,
and Kansas, the fruits and flowers; and the birds—peregrine
falcon, seagull, pheasant, pelican, condor, wren, scissortail
flycatcher—all instead of the bald eagle
clutching a sheaf of arrows.
On the obverse George Washington shows
a lot of skin: his naked neck and shoulder express the mortal
nature of who would not wear an imperial mantle,
laurel wreath, crown of rays, or diadem.
In this he goes against the type: if we trust a god, it isn't him.

II.

There's a reason why it's always a quarter
your oddball uncle pulls out from behind your ear:
his sleights-of-hand reach backwards to the coin
Jesus told the Pharisees to render un-
to Caesar: an aureus, equal to 25 denarii, the image of Augustus on one side,
CAESAR AVGVSTVS DIVI circumscribed,
the difference between the king's real
or his stampèd face effaced when divinity's the coin of the realm.
On the reverse an eagle clutches the world it is larger than.
Frederick II of Hohenstaufen,
ruler of the agglomeration Voltaire
dismissed as "neither holy, nor Roman, nor an empire,"
claimed that as the moment the Lord "looking on the portrait
of the coin for the payment of tribute, indicated in sight
of all other kings, the lofty height of the imperial destiny."
On his coins, Frederick's mantled profile is crowned with rays.
His eagle has retracted her claws, in obedience
to the restraint and tension of the time. Here starts the Renaissance.

III.

Dollar, from *Taler,* abbreviated from Joachimstaler,
from Joachimistal, the valley where silver
was mined, in what is now the Czech Republic and was then
part of the Holy Roman
Empire. Frederick's gold augustales, struck in 1231 in Brindisi
and Messina, assert an unchanged, unchanging authority,
as our two layers of cupronickel on a core of
pure copper, which some anonymous, savage wit dubbed
a Johnson Sandwich, the plentitude of images
of plenty, the scenic scenes, the commemoratives,
imply a trial separation in numismatics' marriage of the practical
and the ideal, or the final valuation of the individual,
so that, like the doubloon Ahab hammered
to the main-mast, the round gold the image of the rounder
globe, which like a magician's glass
to each and every man in turn but mirrors back
his own mysterious self, every one of us will have in time
our own quarter of our own distinct design.

IV.

My quarter would have the pugnacious bearded
shtetl scholar peasant profile of my father, Maury David Feld,
with the legend which did such damage to his career
at Harvard, YOU'VE GOT IT ALL WRONG, and his years,
1924–2005.
What tact I have comes from my mother's side.
This side serves as memorial and warning. On the reverse
I'd have my favorite bird, the northern goshawk, perched
on a Douglas Fir backed by a clear-cut hillside, over-
looking stumps and a small bulldozer.
I would not shy away from the damage done to
the landscape, or the new, more comprehensive view
damage affords. The detailing should be exact
as type and species, genius and family, require: dark skullcap
and cheek, pale eyebrow stripe, an expression
of angry vigilance, pinched by the constriction
of her space, the shrinking old growth on which she stands
facing the open, empty future of our hands.

THERE

Sound of the air's fabric tearing apart,
Of the fire-trees shedding their skins and falling,
Falling in August when the drought of March,
     April, May, June, and July
        Ignites and all the insects come swarming
East, fleeing the burning West. Sound of the Harley-
Davidsons making their pilgrimage to Sturgis
South Dakota, swarming inside I-
90's east-west corridor like fire-maddened insects.

Of the great fire-forests of the West
We say this harvest is the overdue
Returning of the fire-pigeons to their nests,
     That fire-power so long accrued
        Ignites and we become the fire.
So on TV the burning flags are ours
Because they're burning. So on the internet
A woman with a flame painted on each breast
Rides the back of a motorcycle all the way to Sturgis.

A woman with a flame painted on each breast
Looked down at me in my green Honda Civic,
Across the distance actors keep to keep the fiction
     Real. I saw her in a Gulf station
        Talking to the child in her cell phone

As a dozen digital cameras focused in on
Her red, blue, and yellow latex. Then on the internet.
If you close your eyes and touch your laptop screen
It feels like her body-painted skin.

Sweetie, Mommy and Daddy'll be home soon
But now they're riding a full tank of gas
To the Trail of Tears Rest Area parking lot,
      Where there'll be beer and barbeque
      In a vinegar and honey sauce;
The sweet charred meat a burnt offering to
The distance ritual requires us to cross
So we'll arrive annealed as sacred groves passed through
The purifying fire. And Sweetie, we *love* you

But now we're riding our good credit lines across
The mise-en-scène of our indigenous holocaust
To the Trail of Tears Rest Area parking lot,
      Through the Badlands' Brazil-waxed hills
      Where the country's all passed out on pills
And peppermint schnapps, ready for some black-out sex
We'd totally deny if it wasn't on the internet
With captions and disclaimers in four languages.
Les femmes de motards deviennent sauvages!

The Badlands are a picnic table with a Weber Grill
Sunset of ash-gray coals and wet mesquite
Slowly smoking the poorest cuts of meat
      Until the knotted tendons, fat, and gristle
      Dissolve, and from the deepest cells

The long-pent sugars are released, sweet
As the wasp's black honey, which is the axle-grease
Thick wetness of the woman you're having an affair
With. If she's your wife at home, she isn't here.

In the Trail of Tears rest area parking lot
Harley-Davidsons circle like angry wasps
The sweet sewage smelling Porta-Potties
        And the deep-throated thoracic thrum
        Of their Softtails and Dyna Glides
Is the frustration of a million wasps amplified
As they circle around the lily's rim,
By their imperfect mouths' design denied
The deeply-seated nectaries within.

And then the door you've been waiting for opens
To the sour cell of everyone's digestion
And the sweetly perfumed sanitizer.
        Inside my green Civic the air-
        Conditioner blows a cold wind
From November 2004, post-election.
I get good mileage out of my despair.
Under a sky blue as a bottle of Evian
The motorcyclists rev their unmuffled engines.

The sound of their engines is an anthem
You have to hear at the loudest possible volume
To understand. Trust me, you have to be there,
        A cold liter of Vichy Water
        Vibrating in your hand as they sing of Sturgis,

The coals of pollen glowing inside the calyx,
Tasted their empty carbs and carcinogens
And seen the cracks in the fire and her white skin
Showing through in the parking lot outside the Gulf station

As her voice cracks telling the child in her cell phone,
Don't cry, even if the tank and our good credit lines
Run dry we can still coast there on the fumes;
    The greasy highway will take us there
    As borne upon a beetle's wing.
There, the garden is guarded by walls of painted fire.
There, the bud and its blight are one and we *love* our infection.
There, we are the anthem with our flawed mouths we sing.
There, there, Sweetie, don't cry, she said. There. There.

THERE: AN EPISTLE

And when I passed and drove away from there,
The line of motorcycles in my rearview mirror
Veered off the interstate in a smooth arc
Distance streamlined the differences off of, as dark
Levis and leathers blacked out their pale skins
And then their streaming numbers swallowed them.
So the helmetless outlaw with mutton-chops,
Black hair blown behind him like his brain's exhaust,
And the middle-age spreading couple stuffed
In matching Harley outfits, postures stiff
As seated children at a formal dance,
Blended together in a current curved against
The bank of their low-centered gravity.
Sprung free in my determined trajectory
To you, Pimone, I was surprised by a sudden
Odd pang of loss coupled with irritation—
That too-familiar sense of being excluded from
A community I never wished or asked to join.
The butch-regalia'd mob which carried me,
As if borne by an explosion, across three
States where the plains display such reticence
As one ascribes to the sullen self-defens-
Ive plea of an embarrassment of dirt and sky
(*Don't stop, Traveler, don't think: drive on, drive by*)
Cohered into a humming whole, then thinned
Into a fuse by the dun hills tampened

Out completely, as my long westering slog
Passed from epicenter to epilogue.

Belovèd, how in these distances are fixed   ⎞
The cloudy locutions of a rhetoric   ⎬
Enchanted by its own stupid music!   ⎠
How, gliding along, these bikers are paralleled
By larger, iconic versions of themselves
As if they glided down the portrait-hung
Corridor of a great house, a hallway leading
To the horizon-hinge, which opens, and then
You're on the other side of the billboards,
Where there's scaffolding, the road toward
Wyoming, and you feel as if an after-shock
How their great hits trembled our green Civic,
How static amplified becomes applause,
And how South Dakota is to Wyoming as
TV is to the big screen. Kind of a let-down,
Really, how in my rearview Sturgis browned
Out, switchgrass twisted in the trucks' back-draft,
And I was an eye inside an eye, looking back.

When I passed through and was so briefly *there*
All I felt was a sense of lessened pressure,
Not an azure, dream-pulsed awakening
But a kind of leeching-off, a suppuration.

Then, to refute my ill will's sour self-taste
The signs announced my passage to a state
Where different rules applied—no more billboards!

And to enhance that sense of progress toward
An unseen goal borders are for, the highway curved
Through crumpled hills and closely cropped pastures;
The uplands rising to the great divide—
Seen now, as the landscape opened to provide
Sudden, heart-stopping panoramic views
Of peaks the pangs of distance sharpen to
Inverted points of empty, metallic gray
Against, until the road twists me away
From that vision, towards the point of this
Poem, its destination and genesis.
A snapped-off piece of road straight up a hill
Pitched steep as the bucket of sand Lukas will
Dump on the beach, in the now-past future,
And on the margin's dirt like sun-dried leather,
Bird and prey. Alone, on the opposite side
Of all the traffic swarming towards what I'd
Been through, I slowed to 40, 30,
20, 10. Then what at first had seemed only
Part of the casual slaughter of our highways—
crow, hawk, vulture, fawn, doe, stag—and O days
Spent in the in-between, lost, desiring, time's kill—
Revealed itself as a golden eagle
Choking, or claiming by the neck—a goat?
No, knuckled graphite horns: an antelope.
Head twisted around as in *The Exorcist,*
Owl-wise, pink slip of tongue between black lips.
Its animal athleticism, so freshly killed,
Gave to the strip of dirt where its guts spilled
A still-vibrant significance which far

Exceeded the lane of fast-food wrappers,
Piss-filled bottles and stubbled weeds we've left
Allotted to its kind. I felt the death
Blow on my neck, transfixed into the here
And now by what possessively returned my stare,
As the brown bird shrank in my rearview mirror
(I had to move), watching me watch it disappear.

EPILOGUE TO "THERE"

o afterthought   famous backward look
nostalgia   esprit d'escalier   regret
the elegant, elongated neck
gripped in the yellow talons   flinty hooks
receding before me   silver piece   of the past
golden eye   in a fading silhouette
o emblem   of our lost republic
drawing me on in my ascent   a crack
in the eye   wound   I remember here
as   an opening   in my rearview mirror
star   in the forehead   I need to orient
myself   as I continue   my ascent
to a line of mountains   broken bottles on a wall
piled shards   jagged edges   rimed with salt

AFTER JOHNNY CARSON'S FINAL APPEARANCE ON *THE TONIGHT SHOW*

Democracy is the eagle on the back of a dollar bill, with 13 arrows in one claw, 13 leaves on a branch, 13 tail feathers, and 13 stars over its head. This signifies that when the white man came to this country, it was bad luck for the Indians, bad luck for the trees, bad luck for the wildlife, and lights out for the American eagle.
—Johnny Carson, September 11, 1991

There is always some darkness hidden inside the light.
No matter how bright the klieg, the spot, the house—
still some spot, shadow, wisp, or stain.
It is well known that even on the sun there are shadows.

I have talked my whole life as if talking were a kind of light.
I opened my mouth and from behind the shadow of my face
streamed out the kind of conversation they call *light*—
barbed quips, banter, innuendo, mock seriousness. Jokes.

With my last breath I will insist that I was generous
with my light. I gave it to you, my guests,
so we could build between us, out of the silver stain
in your shut eyes after the bulb's flash, a Mylar balloon

filled with your good night breath rising like a sigh
above the grease and gravies, the coffees and highballs
of your day all clean and reflective, a mirror in which
you stop the throat of the woman you are with your penis.

It was never as easy as it looked. There was a cost.
To give you that, I had to kill my self. At first I was afraid—
how terrible, I thought, to be a man with no self.
I couldn't do it. I sat in my dark canyon and measured

my ambitions against my abilities as rain cast its feelers
against my picture windows and the distant traffic
sighed in its famous imitation of Whitman's dark mother.
For the first and last time I looked deep in my heart

and in that bleak scrutiny the child dissolved, weeping.
Among the many things the child weeps for
in his unfathomable self-pity is his lost silver balloon.
That and, you know—*America*. America, it is my pleasure

to give you back your silver balloon. Please don't lose it again.

TONGUE: AN ODE

Tongue doesn't fit in: the only muscle to protrude
into the public arena, a hot flicker of inner meat,
tongue's a piece of work. If an animal, you'd say
it tries to escape from an ivory amphitheater, but
tethers haul it back through worn rubble and sharp
dogs' teeth, to an unlit cell and the open drainage
of the throat. If eyes are the soul's mirror, then
mouth is its cesspit and tongue is trapped between
them and split down the middle, divided into taste
and talk. When tongue speaks in tongue as tongue,
it signifies anxiety, or hunger, or sex, or a dis-
respect, as when Rimbaud's divine master, propping
himself against a column to watch the sons of sin,
sees the demon's tongue sticking out of all their
mouths, or when our leader said look I'm not
gonna lie, it's not gonna be easy, but we'll kill
the Bill of Rights; and slipping out in the pauses
meant to represent thought, this spit-slick member
of his inner constituency, compounded of fiber and
fat. The epithelium is of the scaly variety, like
that of the epidermis. It covers the free surface
and can be detached by maceration or boiling; then
you'll see how tongue's skin is thinner than skin.
If sorrow's controlled by song, then stuttering is
the Ur-elegy, a chain of sounds rattling in grief.

We're sorry, we'd love to talk, but tongue's tied
up in knots right now. My tongue is a thick towel
stalled in the soak cycle, so its Ss stick, and I
talk funny, as I slot four quarters into the silver
tongue of another machine, and hope this time I'll
speak in trumpets or massed angelic choirs. Eating
a grilled turkey on sourdough sandwich, I consider
how my mouth is a cage in which my tongue is a
bird eating another bird, as the dry toasted bread
crunches like the brittle ribs of a thrush. Sharp
is the golden eagle's worn whetstone beak, sharp,
its tongue, curved like a scimitar, the hyoid bone
underneath, and sharp are the series of shrieks of
the caged bird demanding its dinner; and the blade
of its tongue fits perfectly into the beak's stone sheath.

EPICENTRAL

I.

Sunday calls from what once was home: new news
    if any, first, then inquiries. On one
side of the continent, a child's progress,
    careers: back there, health updates, then the slow
erosion of old friends, the vibrant social
    circle I grew in and out of dissolving
under strokes, cancers, Alzheimer's, the loss
    of other vital senses, and the weather
inside Verizon's static'd connection as rain
    hisses the surface of a pond to mist,
a wreckage of zeros on the face of it.

II.

i.

In Kensington, Bethesda, and Silver Springs,
the day opens like an aluminum-
foil envelope filled with crushed aspirin.

ii.

According to the *Times* science section,
the virus killed half the jays, wrens, and robins,
and over 90% of the crows and ravens.

iii.

Calling from Maryland, my father-in-law,
by nature inclined to a brusque reticence,
conceded only a different kind of silence.

iv.

In Kensington, a servant of the state,
Athena's owl on his chest, is watering
his lawn, the owl's eyes two orange rings.

v.

Calling from suburban Maryland, my father-
in-law, by nature an economist,
said squirrel chatter soon filled the emptiness.

vi.

The West Nile virus killed the Corvids,
robins, house wrens, and eastern jays: the nui-
sance birds only a specialist could love.

vii.

In Kensington, Bethesda, and Silver Springs,
the beds are dry: the waters of speech are stilled
as servants of the state wait at their grills.

viii.

From here I can admire his skeptic mind
and how his forced neutrality and restraint
offer a caution in the form of a complaint.

ix.

In Kensington, Bethesda, and Silver Springs,
an analgesic dust proxies the dusk
and night descends like Tylenol PMs.

III.

i.

Visiting a year later, I start to shiver in the CVS
parking lot: the onset of a summer flu unsettling
me further where untenanted air and telephone

wires add erasures to a day already over-exposed,
all shadows peeled off or stolen. At 101 by noon
and rising together, I offer my fever as a challenge

to August, both of us racing to what my chicken-
flesh, shivering under quilts or splayed out to avoid
self-adhesion, feels as a precipice where numbers

dissolve in their own heat with words like *contagion*,
said to be general as on the television a malignancy
with a constituency warns one attacks our foundation.

ii.

Evening and I feel better, but still awful. Against
my forehead in the cool glass of backwards looks
their neighbor washes the sandy features of his face

in white wine, and as he walks his deer-ravaged
rows of tulips drinks, pauses, and pisses, the sound
of his micturition mixed with the soft half-sigh,

half-song some older men breathe for comfort as
they force reluctant water up the urethra, as I heard
issue from my father in an alley in Rome between

prostate surgeries and thought an embarrassment
until the Harpo in my bathroom mirror sang it to me
in our identity dance together, which made it worse.

iii.

From my father I also inherited a Purple Heart,
contempt for the American military officer class,
an uxorious nature, a taste for literary gossip

slash biography, and some excellent Brunellos
slowly aging into my blood type, to be consumed
in a blessèd neutrality. But now, I'm not even

myself. Fevered a few degrees from who pays bills,
reads Merrill, Gunn, Dugan, and Lukas Star Wars books
goodnight, only a smudged lens and waist-high chain

link fence separate me from the neighbor who sprays
flowers deer will eat anyway, pissing away what's left
of an exhausting day on red, orange, and yellow tulips.

iv.

He hopes his scent will frighten off the deer, or tang
of insult make the stag pause as it canters at an angle
into the instant the road kills in. Red flares through

the greenery between us and the parkway as rush hour
stalls around the broken neck, antlers and the blood-shot
twist of tube protruding from the anus, as the full weight

of what he raced animal steps ahead of stills the brown,
white-tipped deer-hide to dusk's colorlessness, wherein
our neighbor walks and sings his absent-minded song

as he turns to ash, and in the living room my son explains
how new battles are better than old ones, gravely followed
by my wife, and I resolve to honor the living, not the life.

Three

"A Slaughter at Cape May"

From the Journals of John and Frank (Ages Seventeen)

It certainly was awful to see the hunters shoot down every Sharp-shinned Hawk that came along. We thought that just about 90% of the Sharpshins that crossed the road on Saturday were killed, although only about 40% on Friday, when it was so windy. I saw some of the hunters who used duck loads and a 32-inch barrel hit hawks at a hundred yards above them. While back at camp we would watch a hawk as he passed us and went toward the road. We would say, "There goes another one, watch them get him," and they usually did. Sometimes it would take five or six shots to get a big Cooper's Hawk but they came down in the end. They were mostly from up north and had no fear of man, which made the slaughter even worse. John saw a man shoot a hawk out of a tree with a shotgun, never even giving him a sporting chance. Shells were piled all over the road and hawks were piled all over the running boards of cars and scattered throughout the woods, for no one bothered getting a hawk that fell anywhere but in the road. When we think that these are not only hawks from New Jersey but from all over the Northeastern United States and Canada, it seems a crime that they should be slaughtered.

Among all the hawks we saw, not one was a mature bird. I would like to know whether old hawks migrate or whether they migrate by a different route or at a different time. I would like to know the reason for their gathering together in bunches over this one spot.

Hawks in the Hand, Frank and John Craighead

· HYBRID IMPRINT

Screaming, screaming for days until someone
    called the police, the bird presented itself
as all kinds of problems, caught near the top
    of a pretty monstrous red cedar. Trying to place
the voice, our crew sorted out their equipment
    in the pasture, one man apart, gazing upward
in what looked like abstraction as he mapped
    his route through the tangled intelligence
of the crown. Even with spikes, ropes and ladders,
    soft words, and a net, the bird would be a bitch
to get down, to free, meaning, to capture.
    That they were wrong was another problem.
Hunger dociles a bird, but the way this falcon
    took to his glove once he'd unsnagged
the eyelet of his or her polypropylene jesses
    from the twig was over-familiar,
like a passenger returning from rough seas
    to land. And the falcon kept nagging
at him, screaming, as it had no other speech.

Up close, the thing taxed their taxonomy, who
    by trade, by calling, know each genus
and species—a falcon, yes, but not one they'd seen;
    until their expert identified it as a peregrine/
gyrfalcon hybrid, a bird manufactured to combine
    the speed of one with the bulk of the other.

Arctic white on its under-wings and breast, Peregrinest
    about the tail and back, the head kind of
a botch, rippled with brown and white like drops
    of coffee on a tablecloth its alert
scanning seemed an effort to shake off; the bird
    was impressive, the size of a wine bottle
and weighing as much as intoxication. Ads would
    be taken out, calls made, messages left
on appropriate forums; all received no response.
    There is a famous embarrassment falconers
feel about losing a bird; or maybe this one
    had proven more trouble than could be handled.

An imprint, a bird which thinks it's human,
    raised wrongly or by intent, lacks
the instinctual caution of its kind, will attack
    dogs and handlers, has *boundary issues*,
expresses fellow-feeling in the form of aggression,
    renders all questions of wild or tame
specious. The confused son of our calculations—
    by now we knew, by size and by temperament,
it was a he—part science, part engineering,
    part love, part sport, part the sport of
its making, bastarded out of every other bird's
    unquestionable rightness of function
and place, the hybrid is a perfect machine
    that naturally the world has no use for,
as innocent as anything which kills can be.
    Since we are as close to its kind
as any other, we brought the bird home,
    calling it *Edmund*, which is my middle name.

POST-CONFESSIONAL

Yesterday I dropped and broke the fountain pen
You gave me—an expensive gift: a Pelikan.
The little death of its black ejaculation,

A spray of dots across the hardwood floor
Like seeds of the unwritten, smeared over
The surface of the wavy grain. Water

Just thinned and spread the stain. At Matthews Beach
I locked the keys in the car. Dangling out of reach,
Like a far mountain range, the bitten teeth

Impressed themselves into the soft tissue
The sky's gray matter-of-factness floated through:
Today will be like a punishment for you.

Then at the afternoon play-date your friend
Behind whose house in busy hives twelve heron-
Couples brought out-sized life into the barren

Branches where our March paused, a broken clock
Elaborately painted, or iconographic
Image, folk art, lacking perspective, the shock

Of how last week, she said, a juvenile
Bald eagle went through the tree, devouring all
The eggs. The heron pairs shrieked through the awful

Morning, then left for what she called Forever.
Why do we feel implicated in this? We are
Grounded in local knowledge: the kitchen counter,

Mosaic back-splash you wanted me to see
(Not impressed), the little shelf of self I need,
Precarious perch, to stand on when I speak.

The bald eagle, if you've been alone with one—
You haven't but I have is what I mean—
Is a nasty piece of work, its voice the lonesome

Aphasiac twittering of an entitled seagull,
A smaller nuisance-bird much like the eagle,
Absent the majesties of flight. As symbol

The eagle diminishes any amount of sky
Down to a stamp or coin and reifies
Itself with such an imperial dignity I

Feel embarrassed when one flies overhead
By how little I feel, so totally unstirred.
The bald eagle is no longer endangered

Because *symbol* is worth much more than *image*.
Above motors the streamlined fuselage:
The Cruciform shadow wavers below. The caged

Eagle McKenzie fluted with panic as she fell,
Crippled wings spread eagle-wise and talons
Outstretched, as pictured on the dollar bill:

First the impact, like being hit with a pillow
Case full of broken glass, then the cracked open
Aquarium smell of algae and gravel flowed

Up my arm from the hurt, which arrived last,
After the insulating layer of unlikeness
Between us reasserted itself. I flushed the gash

Out with disinfectant, though I still bear
The flash-mark of our contact on my arm near
The more straightforward, self-inflicted scars

Of my lunatic twenties. Who was that person?
Medicated out of my bipolar spectrum
Illness, safely diagnosed, I'm off to Home

Depot for screens and paint in our new car.
I have a mortgage, a son, and am unfathered.
Some idiots keep sending me credit cards.

I bought an even better Pelikan.
Imprisoned by her injuries, you'd think even
A crippled eagle would have a decent sense

Of balance. Here on my arm is where you're wrong.
McKenzie lurches away from me, up the gang-
Plank to her perch. White head, slumped shoulders, going

Back to the plastered nest we built for her,
So like the way in his last weeks my father
Returned to bed, pushing his wheeled stroller,

Saying in his strict Epicureanism
That since he could no longer live without pain
He would no longer live. It was his decision.

GUIDE

All summer we could feel the pressure building
as the contagion stalled in Siskiyou,
against the High Cascades, and out of fear
we draped the cages with mosquito netting,
so even on the sharpest days our birds
lived in a dull half-light that hid their wounds
and blurred their distinctive markings. So carrying in
a defrosted rat with a smear of vitamins
like mold on its wet, white belly, I thought
the shadow the approaching virus cast
a kind of willed obscurity, as if a brush
had been dragged across the wet, pigment-
loaded surface of a photorealist landscape.
Outside, the studious children pressed close
to the fence in their matching day-camp T-shirts,
each one holding a small handful of shade
over their eyes or squinting through the mask
brilliantly applied to their morning faces.
With a kinked, self-entangled hose spitting
at the joints and a clipboard of my tasks, I led
the little yellow-shirted mob up and down
the Center's steep-pitched precincts, giving each cage
a plaque of description as I dragged in
the coils and washed away the chalky mutes,
returning to the mild reproach of their silence
and sun-shocked stares with a swatch of rodent pelt

or leathery viscera in my latexed hand.
How strange I must have seemed to them! a bald man
inside a veiled box talking about
the *Silent Spring* and loss of habitat,
and how the kestrel's ultra-violet vision
can see the trail of vole urine but not
the power line that interrupts its flight,
as he fed an injured shadow with a voice
like a rusted hinge and a rending appetite.
From kestrel to kite they followed me, goshawk,
osprey, and vulture, pygmy to spotted owl,
until we reached the gravel turnaround
where by the minivans their parents waited,
knotted in tight social clusters, and where
as a form of farewell, to give these brilliant kids
a less approximate sense of what their strained sight
had guessed toward, I brought one of our display birds,
Taka, a Swainson's hawk, out of its cage.
Released from the necessary constrictions
of its mesh-covered enclosure into the open
extremities of summer air, the dark
morph male had a conniption fit, yo-yoing
against his jesses toward and away from
the closing-in circle of day-campers,
who were also scared and excited. Children,
that fluttering you feel in the muscles outside the ribs
over your heart as the bird I hold out to you
opens his wings, which are dark gray and brown
like dry, weather-worn shingles, and with the sound
of a dishrag shaken clean threatens to break
his splintery pinions on the air between us,

is how your bodies would redress a wound
older than you, by taking off my hand
that portion of his weight that is the fear
he has instead of marrow in his bones.
To soothe the hawk I sang the lullaby
we use at feeding times to call our birds
to glove. The song is archaic but it works
as a point of contact between us and allows
an allotment of freedom like the length
of jess between swivel and anklet Taka tests
as he treads along the forefinger of my
double-thick goatskin glove, eyeing the children
with a look of fiercely prim skepticism
as they disperse into their parents' cars
to be belted into their booster seats.

CASCADE RAPTOR CENTER: RELEASE

for Nick and Robyn

Please tell me why, exactly, would anyone choose
to have a child?

There were instructions, to reach in and grab the feet,
to pull the hawk out of the box, then to provide what-
ever kind of blessing the occasion asks of you as you
release.

Would you say this was a moral *decision?*

Of course the bird had no use for our wordy protocol.
At the opening she burst from the box, sprung back to
her previous life, returning healed, or only minimally
scarred.

That hardly seems enough.

Something borrowed from the blue, something stolen,
maimed, made whole and then returned, a little patch
on the sky to signify not everything we touch turns to
crap.

Okay. Take me through this.

Since most are so much the worse for any encounter
with us, we celebrate when one survives. Nick in his

office editing EMT films, increasingly wolf. Pimone teaching.

The pet-box in the back seat with ventilation holes and a carrying handle, the bird rising out with the sound of a present unwrapping.

Too vague. Some details, please?

The flight cage, off-limits, the mice in the open-roofed pen. *The general public may, quite justifiably, find the idea of bagged game revolting.* The distressed rabbits, crying.

The hole in the wing, the impact, the bullet bearing our imprint connecting the bird to the barrel, the explosion, the kick, the punctured primer, the firing pin, the pulled trigger.

The being born, the blood-sugars monitored, the insulin injected into the stomach, the first-trimester Zofran and the pillows next to the toilet, the pre-natal vitamins.

Was it worth it?

The last and largest spiral bearing the red-tailed hawk out of our sight, into a sky altered for us by the addition of a few molecules bearing our imprint, a sky inhabited, alive.

RAPTOR

The effort required to keep the neck-snapped hare
Above the spears of cordgrass prickling the mudflats where
The estuary runs aground: in the August brilliance of
His second summer's coat, the tercel fell like love
Through the empty, intersecting avenues of air
To touch the browsing rabbit on the soft spot
Where the nervous skullful of rabbit-thought
And the hunched hurry of rabbit-muscle meet:
There the peregrine punched with balled-up feet,
Then hopped and hung, a burnished blue-gray burr
Lodged in the day's clear sight,
Until its wings, fluttering like eyelids, caught flight
And we could see in our binoculars
The tipping point where half-thought, half-inclination,
Becomes a blade careering to one end,
As the trap of narrative the falcon labors in
Sprung shut, capturing a precise portion of this
Too bright, emblazoned day, so that the disc,
Black-bordered inside our trembling hands,
In which on a burnt pine branch a falcon stands
Over its shadow as a greasy yellow string
Of rabbit-gut, ratcheted inch by dangling
Inch up into its beak, is a device
Heraldic in its figuration and precise
As the infinitesimal calibrations of fear, which wake
Me night-soaked next to your comforted shape;

As you sleep with a mask on I would not lift
Only to vex you further, and the falcon still in its
Precipitous decline stares back at me, each flick
Of his dark-hooded head keeping a sclerotic-
Ringed eye on the distance between us,
Which is absolute, and which if we tried to cross
He would escape into, taking with him the hunger
He is instrument and of air, the song, the measure.

THE TEST

California Hawking Club Apprentice Study Guide, Frederick W. "Rick" Holderman, editor

1) **True or false:** Falconry hawks are trained to accept humans as their master and owner.
2) **True or false:** Hawks should not be made too tame but should be encouraged to retain their wild nature.

1) **False.** The point of falconry is to teach the hawk that hunting with one specific human leads to eating better than hunting alone in the wild.
2) **False.** Tameness is a point of refinement in the art of falconry, and serves as a measure of the confidence and trust she has in you.

For months I was stuck in Eugene,
    stalled on how in the five centuries
        between
But they that somtyme lykt my companye
Like lyse awaye from ded bodies thei crall:
        and
But they that sometime liked my company
Like lice away from dead bodies they crawl
        the lice blanched into grains
        of rice scattered around a body
            only dressed to be killed,
        and how these college towns depress
your serotonin reuptake inhibitors,
    as the rain slows to a thick mist
and an air like Ambien gums up your neurons.

Match diseases with treatment:

apoplexy   Flagyl/Spartrix
bumblefoot   Pepto-Bismol/Pedialyte
cramps   chelating agents
frounce   sugar water
lead poisoning sunlight/vitamin D3/vitamin B
seizures   a variety of clean perches
sour crop   ground up bones in food
stargazing   a cool dark place and medical attention

Translate the following passage:

I went to the birds then,
          for a language archaic as needed
and scientific as necessary,
          for the shrill, screaming music
they are, and their elaborate syntax
          of muscle and feather,
for the peregrine's **roused** plumage
          in the **mews** as she **bowses**
from a bowl of bath water or how
          when she **bates** on my glove
her slate gray-blue wings strobe
          over her pale barred breast
and her **flying weight** flutters
          against the jesses,
for how the goshawk in **yarak**
          bows forward, as if straining
against bad eyesight to read
          the distance until **slipped**,

for how the Cooper's hawk **towers**
    over the field it is hard-wired to
as doves and robins **sky-up**,
    for how the red-tail of my
apprenticeship after **breaking in**
    the cottontail she was **wedded to**,
returned to my fist
    to **preen** and to **feak**.

Glossary:

Rouse, to: When a hawk stands all her feathers on end at once and gives them a rattling shake. A sign of well being.
Mews: Any place where a hawk is kept at night or in bad weather.
Bowse, to: Drinking by a hawk. Hence boozer and boozing.
Bate, to: The wild jumping off and beating of wings while still held to perch or fist. May be caused by wildness, fright, boredom or plain temper.
Flying weight: The weight at which the hawk is healthy enough to fly and hunt, yet sufficiently hungry to respond to the falconer's control. Also sharp set, keen and combat weight.
Yarak: an Indian term describing a savage state of extreme readiness to kill. A hawk in yarak adopts a certain unique posture which makes it appear especially dangerous.
Slip: A chance at quarry. **To slip:** to release a hawk in pursuit of quarry.
Tower, to: when a hawk rings up into the air vertically.
Sky-up, to: When a flock of birds take to the air in a flurry to escape an accipiter.
Break in: the act of breaking through a kill's skin, usually starting at the soft underbelly.

Wedded to: When a hawk prefers one kind of quarry.
Preen: When a hawk straightens its feathers by oiling and dressing them.
Feak, to: When a hawk cleans her beak after feeding, wiping it briskly
back and forth. A sign of great confidence if she will do this on your
finger or glove.

For how the bird, my pleasure, my leisure, my captive,
        unhitches for a brief interval from my grasping

to serve as *that tenuous arch linking us to the inaccessible,*
        and then returns to my fist, for how their flat brains

stop our spinning projections into framed photographs,
        eyes packed with receptor cells, two and half times

more accurate than ours, half of the peregrine's brown-
        black stare more than equal to my contemplation,

wild and reserved, remote even as she takes food from
        my hand, the feet perfect for killing and carrying

the kill so we distinguish them by this excellence, and for
        this strange accord reached with a thing of the air,

that they can leave when they choose, but choose to stay.

THE HUNT

I'm sorry you want
to sleep in your
warm pelt for
another hour or two

come out come out
in your crumpled bag
of fur your ears
stiff it's November

the air so empty
it fills your lungs
to the corner
you backed into black

eyes blinking the dirt
our boots shake loose
away the fear
the chill you feel

we share come out
my love my leisure
sniff the air
little one we've come

to kill we smell
good we soap we
shave we shower
little one I'd like

to soothe but fear
keeps you alive a
little longer where
are your little ones

my pet my hunger
they're here come out
come out we're
ready when you are

RAPTOR: A BRIEF LEXICON

Falconry The falconer's primary aspiration should be to possess hunting birds that he has trained through his own ingenuity to capture the quarry he desires in the manner he prefers. The actual taking of prey should be a secondary consideration.

The Art of Falconry

Gorge [(O)Fr. = throat f. Proto-Romance alt. of L *gurges* whirlpool.] 1 The external throat; the front of the neck. *arch.* LME. 2 The internal throat. Now only *rhet.* LME. 3 Orig. in *Falconry*, (the contents of) the crop of a hawk. Now *gen.*, the contents of the stomach (chiefly in phrs. below). LME. s4 A meal, *esp.* (in *Falconry*) for a hawk. Long *rare*.

My falcon now is sharp and passing empty,
And till she stoop she must not be full-gorg'd
The Taming of the Shrew (4.1. 177–78)

Haggard 1 Of a hawk: caught after having assumed its adult plumage; wild, untamed. *fig.* a wild, intractable person. **b** of plumage: ragged. *rare*.

If I do prove her haggard,
Though that her jesses were my dear heartstrings,
I'd whistle her off and let her down the wind
To prey at fortune.
Othello (3.3.259–62)

Jesses. *n.* Narrow straps of leather attached to a hawk's legs, by which she is held. When on the fist these leather straps are held between the fingers.

Mute Of a bird, esp. a hawk: discharge (feces), the action of defecating by a bird, esp. a hawk; *sing* and in *pl.* (a deposit of) feces, droppings.

Peregrine Of the peregrine (implicitly female), Turbervile (1575) notes:
the seconde [after the falcon gentle in a list] is the Haggart
Falcon, whiche is otherwise tearmed the Peregrine Falcon.
"Peregrine" is strongly adjectival here, meaning in effect (according to this writer) from unknown or distant parts, or wanderer, or (oddly) suggestive of "beautie and excellencie."

Raptor [L, f. as RAPT a.: see–OR] **1** *Ornith.* = *bird of prey* s.v. BIRD *n.* LME. **2** A plunderer, a robber. LME–E18. See **Rapt:** Long *poet. rare.* **1** Carry away by force. L16 **2** Transport in spirit; enrapture. Removed from one place or situation to another. Now *poet.*

Seeling
Come seeling night,
Scarf up the tender eye of pitiful day.
Macbeth (3.2.46–47)

Tercel or GENTLE *n.* Also spelled tassel *Shakes.* The male of any variety of hawk, as distinguished from the female, generally called *falcon.* The name is probably derived from the belief that the former is one-third smaller than the latter.